Glaciers
Landscape Carvers

T0362774

Contents

By Lily Erlic

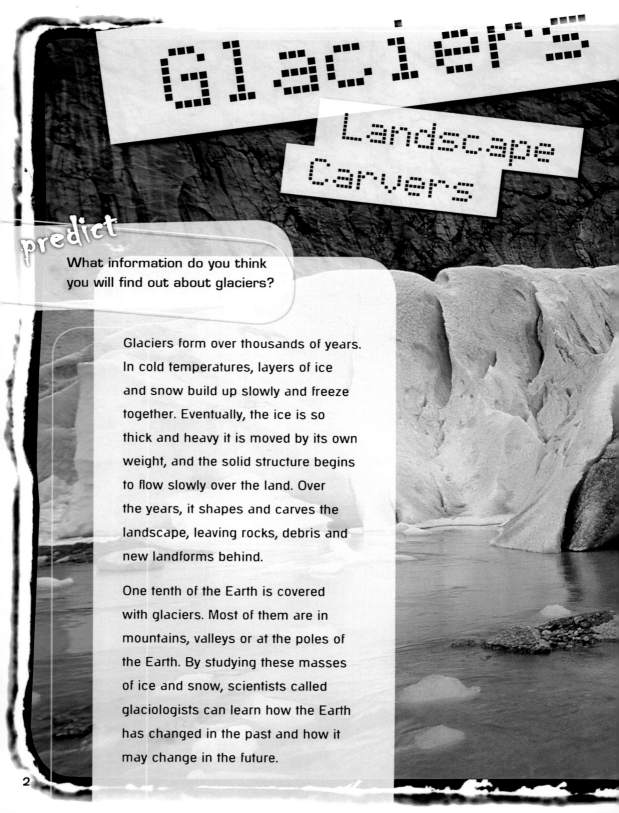

Glaciers
Landscape Carvers

predict

What information do you think
you will find out about glaciers?

Glaciers form over thousands of years.
In cold temperatures, layers of ice
and snow build up slowly and freeze
together. Eventually, the ice is so
thick and heavy it is moved by its own
weight, and the solid structure begins
to flow slowly over the land. Over
the years, it shapes and carves the
landscape, leaving rocks, debris and
new landforms behind.

One tenth of the Earth is covered
with glaciers. Most of them are in
mountains, valleys or at the poles of
the Earth. By studying these masses
of ice and snow, scientists called
glaciologists can learn how the Earth
has changed in the past and how it
may change in the future.

clarify

landforms

word origin

glacier

Where's it from?

3

How Glaciers Form

Glaciers form when snow that falls during the winter does not all melt in the summer. The snow that is left behind slowly builds up in layers over many years.

In the atmosphere, snow crystals, or snowflakes, are tiny hexagonal shapes – like needles or stars. When the snow falls onto the ground, the crystal shapes change as bits evaporate off their sharp points. In this way, the crystals are rounded off and fit more closely together.

As the weight of fallen snow increases, the snow crystals under the surface become more and more compact. They become hard, grain-like pellets called firn. When the firn is buried even deeper under another fall of snow, it is compressed further into dense crystals of glacial ice.

Air spaces between the grains are sealed off and the tiny air bubbles are squeezed out. The ice gradually becomes impermeable to liquids. At great depths it is pure ice.

This process of snow turning to dense glacial ice can happen in three to four years in warmer, wetter areas. The melting and refreezing of liquid makes everything happen faster. On the cold, dry Antarctic plateau, the process takes several thousand years.

clarify

impermeable

dense

snow crystal

Cause and Effect Chart: How Glaciers Form

Cause: **?**

Effect: Snow builds up.

Cause: Snow crystals change shape when they hit the ground.

Effect: **?**

Cause: Weight of snow increases.

Effect: Snow crystals compact into firn.

Cause: More snow falls.

Effect: Firn is buried deeper and is compacted into dense ice.

Visual Challenge
In what other ways could you present this information?

...the process takes several thousand years.

How do you think glaciologists know this?

hexagonal

plateau

Where are they from?

layers of glacial ice (the coloured stripe is debris from an aeroplane crash more than 25 years ago)

There are several different types of glaciers that form. The two main types are continental glaciers and mountain or valley glaciers.

Continental Glaciers

A continental glacier is made up of a broad sheet of thick ice, built up at the centre and sloping slightly outwards in every direction. It can cover up to 5000 square metres near the poles of the Earth.

The zone of accumulation is the place on the glacier where the snow gathers. This is the highest part of the glacier, at the centre of the ice sheet. The zone of ablation is the part of a glacier where the snow and ice melt and evaporate.

Continental glaciers can cover an entire landscape except for the highest mountains. The largest of this type of glacier is called an ice sheet. Ice sheets are found in Antarctica and Greenland. Smaller continental glaciers, such as those in Iceland, are called ice caps.

Greenland ice sheet

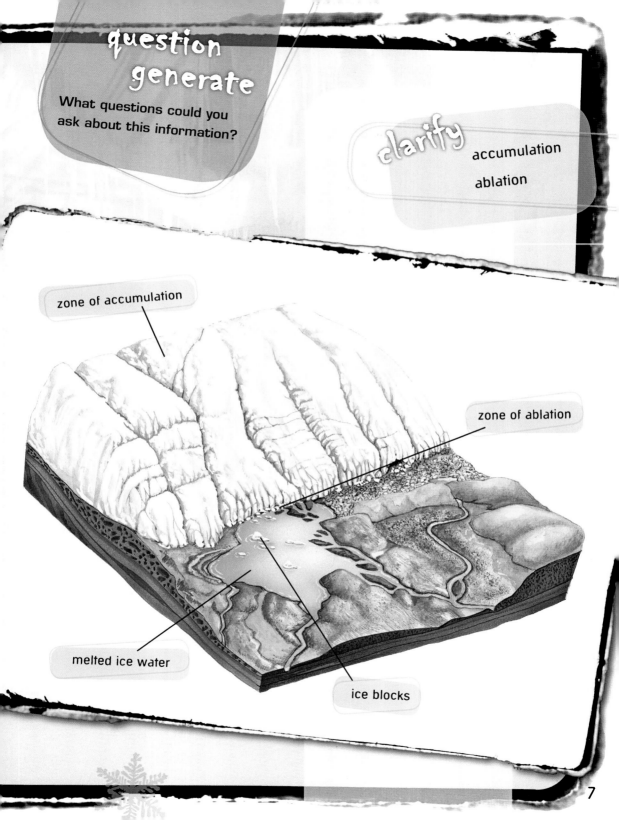

clarify

accumulation

ablation

zone of accumulation

zone of ablation

melted ice water

ice blocks

zone of accumulation

debris moved by the glacier

zone of ablation

They carve out shapes in the mountain-sides as they move...

What can you infer about the effect of glaciers on the landscape?

Valley or Mountain Glaciers

Valley or mountain glaciers are long, narrow bodies of ice found in high mountain valleys. They carve out shapes in the mountain-sides as they move.

Sometimes several glaciers moving downhill come together. However, they remain separate masses and flow on their own.

Some mountains that have these glaciers are the Rockies and the Sierra Nevadas in the US, the Alps in Europe and the Southern Alps in New Zealand. These glaciers can even be found near the Equator, such as in the Andes of South America, or Kenya and Uganda in Africa. However, they are found at very high altitudes where the temperatures are very cold.

Other Glaciers

Cirque glaciers form in bowl-shaped hollows, or cirques, with steep sides cut out of the mountain by the ice. If they become large enough, they move down sloping mountain valleys to become valley glaciers.

When a mountain glacier extends down towards the coastline, it can create a fiord glacier. A fiord is a river valley that has been deeply gouged by glacier ice and then flooded by the sea.

Piedmont glaciers are found at the base of mountains. They form when mountain glaciers flow down onto flatter ground. The ice spreads out into a rounded lump.

piedmont glacier

word origin

cirque

fiord

piedmont

Where are they from?

cirque glacier

fiord glacier

How Glaciers Move

As glaciers form, the ice eventually becomes so thick that it moves under the pressure of its own weight. Most glaciers move slowly, less than 30 centimetres a day. The process is so slow that it is difficult for anyone to see that the ice is moving at all.

There are two ways that glaciers can move. The first is by sliding. Pressure from the heavy layers of ice causes some ice to melt into water underneath the glacier. This water, called meltwater, helps slide the glacier along the ground.

Glaciers can also move by creeping. Pressure from the top ice breaks the deeper ice into layers. The layers can then glide or creep over each other, making the whole glacier move. The thicker the glacier, the faster it will move.

question

Why do you think a thicker glacier would move faster?

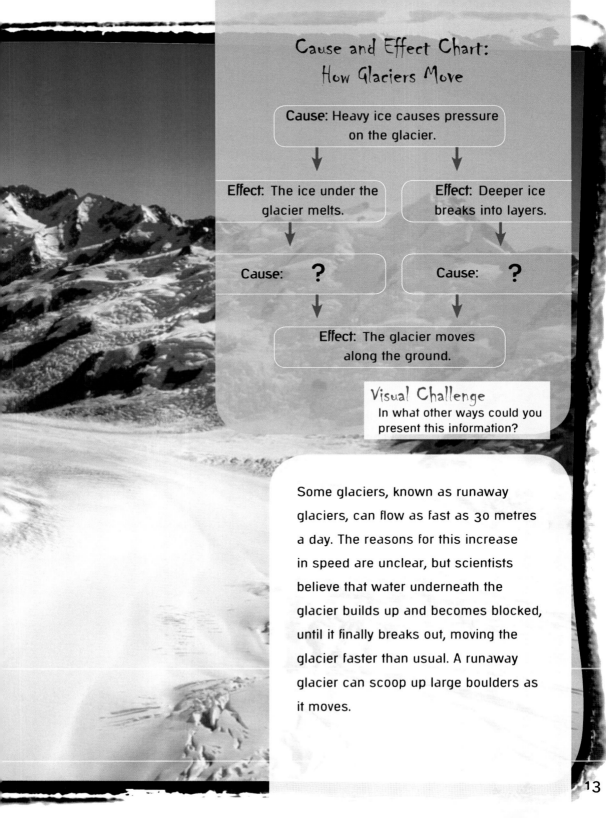

Cause and Effect Chart: How Glaciers Move

Cause: Heavy ice causes pressure on the glacier.

Effect: The ice under the glacier melts.

Effect: Deeper ice breaks into layers.

Cause: ?

Cause: ?

Effect: The glacier moves along the ground.

Visual Challenge
In what other ways could you present this information?

Some glaciers, known as runaway glaciers, can flow as fast as 30 metres a day. The reasons for this increase in speed are unclear, but scientists believe that water underneath the glacier builds up and becomes blocked, until it finally breaks out, moving the glacier faster than usual. A runaway glacier can scoop up large boulders as it moves.

predict

What do you think this information will be about?

Glaciers can advance or retreat. When they advance, they increase in size. When they retreat, they decrease in size.

Glaciers advance or retreat for various reasons. They are affected by changes in temperature and snowfall as the seasons change. Most glaciers increase slightly in the winter. They may also be affected by long-term climate change. The ice sheet covering Greenland, for example, is growing smaller because of a gradual increase in temperature since the early 1900s.

In areas away from the poles, rising summer temperatures can cause surface melting on the glaciers.

In the frozen polar regions the ice sheets retreat from their edges as they meet the sea. As the ice melts, blocks of ice often fall from the front of the glacier and into the sea. This is called calving. It happens very quickly, and a booming sound can be heard as the ice breaks off.

Parts of the ice sheet that have broken away, or calved, can float on the ocean. The calved piece of ice becomes an iceberg.

inference

What can you infer about the effects of seasons on glaciers?

calving

an iceberg

How Glaciers Change the Landscape

When glaciers melt or move across land, they can create new landforms.

When ice sheets melt, they can leave behind large blocks of ice in the loose rocks. That ice then melts, leaving a round hollow called a kettle hole. A kettle hole can be up to 10 metres deep. Many have filled up with water over the years and become swamps or lakes.

When mountain glaciers move and melt, they leave behind deposits of soil and rock. These deposits form ridges called moraines along the sides and front of the glacier.

An esker is a long, narrow ridge of sand and gravel left by a stream of water running under a melting glacier. Some eskers are up to 80 metres high. Their length can vary by hundreds of kilometres.

kettle lakes

word origin

moraine

Where is it from?

esker

moraines

Cause and Effect Chart: How Kettle Lakes Form

Cause: Ice sheet melts.

↓

Effect: **?**

↓

Cause: Blocks of ice melt.

↓

Effect: Kettle hole is left behind.

↓

Cause: **?**

↓

Effect: A kettle lake forms

Visual Challenge
In what other ways could you present this information?

u-shaped valley

crevasse

Where is it from?

horn

cirque

crevasse

moraines

u-shaped valley

kettle lake

esker

a landscape during and after a glacier

18

When a glacier flows over uneven or steep ground, cracks called crevasses can open in the hard upper layer of the ice. These crevasses can be as deep as 60 metres. Glaciologists climb into crevasses with special equipment to study the glacier. They have to be careful not to slip on the ice. Ice water also showers down on the glaciologists from above. But the most dangerous part of going into a crevasse is that the glacier could shift and close the opening while they are still inside.

Glaciers also dig out cirques near the peaks of mountains. Cracks within a cirque are filled with snow and ice that freezes, melts and refreezes. This causes pieces of rock to fall away from the mountain, forming a sunken area. Many cirques can form around the top of a mountain, shaping it into horns. The most famous example of this is the Matterhorn in Switzerland.

U-shaped valleys are formed when a glacier gouges its way down a mountain, leaving a "U" shape when the ice melts. This process takes many thousands of years. The sides of the valley are steep and the bottom is flat.

crevasse

the Matterhorn

inference

What can you infer about the type of job a glaciologist might have?

19

Studying Glaciers

Glaciers can teach scientists a lot about the history of the Earth. All glaciers are affected by changes in the climate around them, particularly changes in temperature and precipitation.

When a glacier moves, advances or retreats, it leaves marks on the landscape. By studying the marks or features made by the glacier, glaciologists can learn about climate changes in the past.

Glaciologists can also study glaciers by looking at satellite photos. The photos are taken every year and compared from year to year, so that the changes in the glaciers can be seen.

The glaciologists work out the size of the glacier by calculating its height and area. They can use this information to make predictions about future climate change.

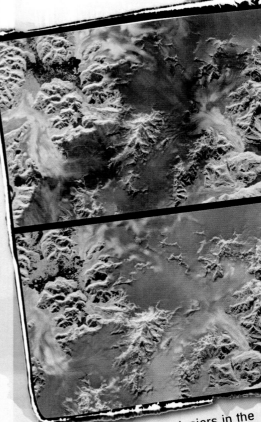

Two radar images of glaciers in the Andes mountains, taken at different times of the year.

question

How do you think glaciologists are able to predict climate change by looking at satellite photos of glaciers?

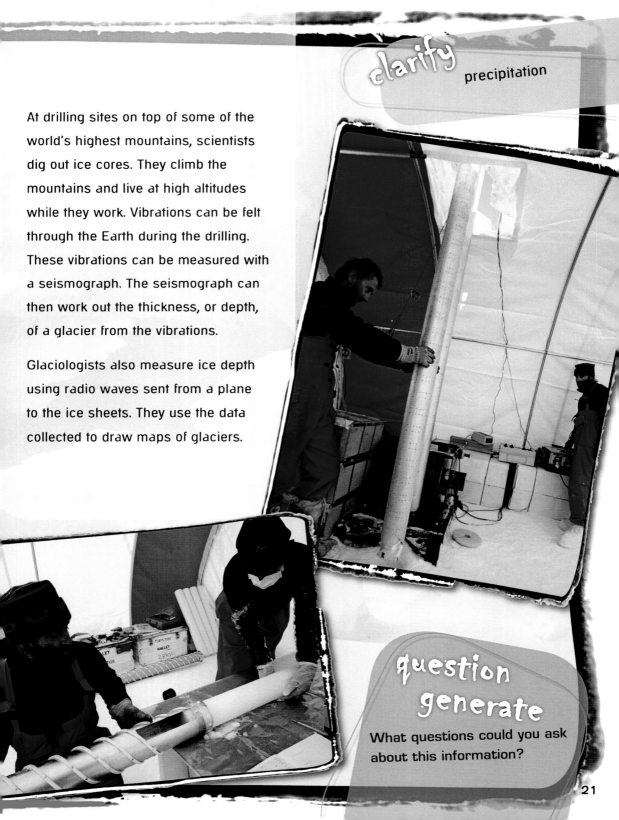

At drilling sites on top of some of the world's highest mountains, scientists dig out ice cores. They climb the mountains and live at high altitudes while they work. Vibrations can be felt through the Earth during the drilling. These vibrations can be measured with a seismograph. The seismograph can then work out the thickness, or depth, of a glacier from the vibrations.

Glaciologists also measure ice depth using radio waves sent from a plane to the ice sheets. They use the data collected to draw maps of glaciers.

question generate

What questions could you ask about this information?

21

clarify   insulated

question

Why do you think the scientists wear clean uniforms, surgical masks and gloves?

The ice cores collected by the glaciologists are loaded into the cargo bay of an aircraft and held in insulated cardboard boxes. They are then flown to storage rooms where scientists can take samples and study the ice. The rooms where the ice cores are stored need to have a temperature between -30°C and -35°C, so that the samples won't melt.

Each sample contains a store of information about the history of the Earth. The scientists examine the ice wearing clean uniforms, surgical masks and gloves.

Through chemical analysis of the ice layers laid down by each winter snowfall, scientists can determine winter temperatures over many years. Cores extracted in Greenland in the early 1990s cover a period of nearly 200,000 years.

By examining tiny bubbles of air trapped in the ice, scientists can gather information about the chemical make-up of the atmosphere when each layer of snow fell.

Scientists also look at pollutants in the ice to find out about the atmosphere. For example, an erupting volcano emits carbon dioxide into the air. Carbon dioxide is also produced when people burn forests or fossil fuels. By measuring carbon dioxide levels in the ice samples, scientists can find out more about when and where volcanoes have erupted and the effects of human activity on the Earth's climate.

close-up of an ice core

inference

Each sample contains a store of information about the history of the Earth...

What can you infer from this?

Ice-core data collected and studied by scientists is now showing that the Earth is warming and the glaciers are melting at a faster rate than ever before. Sea levels are rising at about 2 millimetres a year. Some of this rise is thought to be caused by melting glaciers, particularly mountain glaciers, which are more sensitive to changes in temperature.

Arctic and Antarctic wildlife have been affected by changes on the ice, and polar bears can be seen coming inland when the ice melts.

Melting glaciers can be devastating for people, too. Rivers can flood, causing death and devastation as houses and buildings are destroyed and crops and farm animals swept away or drowned.

More gradual changes caused by rising sea levels can also affect people. As coastlines retreat and settled land is slowly submerged, homes and cultivated land disappear underwater.

inference

What can you infer about the effects of melting glaciers on wildlife in the Arctic and Antarctic?

Experts predict that melting glaciers could be devastating for places prone to flooding, such as Bangladesh.

This lake in Montana, US, was a solid glacier only 60 years ago.

The Earth has been through many periods of freezing and thawing in the past and there have been long periods of time when it was largely ice-free. Glaciers began forming in the Antarctic about 35 million years ago, but trees could still grow there up until about 5 million years ago.

The most recent ice age was 18,000 years ago, during what is known as the last Ice Age. Glacial ice covered about 30 per cent of the world's land area. Vast glaciers and sheets of ice scooped out the basins of the Great Lakes in North America and changed the courses of major rivers such as the Mississippi. Sea levels dropped by as much as 120 metres and parts of what is now ocean floor were dry land.

Today, the Earth is between ice ages, in what is called an interglacial period.

Scientists are still trying to understand why the Earth has ice ages. Most believe that they are related to the gravitational pull of other planets on the Earth. This alters the amount of heat the Earth receives from the sun. Many also believe that the amount of carbon dioxide in the atmosphere has a significant effect on long-term climate changes.

Cause and Effect Chart: Human Effect on Glaciers

Cause: Human activity produces too much carbon dioxide.

↓

Effect: Earth is warming.

↓

?

Visual Challenge
In what other ways could you present this information?

The Great Lakes in North America were formed by glaciers in the last Ice Age.

Index

Think about the Text

Making connections – what connections can you make to the information presented in **Glaciers: Landscape Carvers**?

making discoveries

not having control

learning about something new

Text to Self

caring for the environment

being affected by change

fearing natural disasters

Text to Text

Talk about other informational texts you may have read that have similar features. Compare the texts.

Text to World

Talk about situations in the world that might connect to elements in the text.

Planning an Informational Explanation

1 Select a topic that explains why something is the way it is or how something works.

2 Make a mind map of questions about the topic.

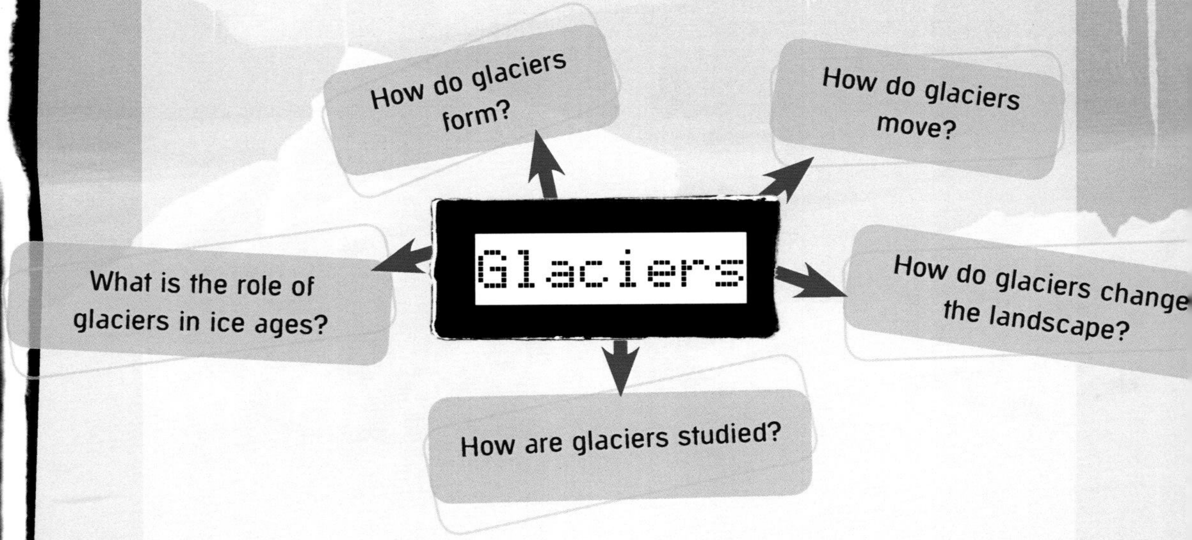

How do glaciers form?

How do glaciers move?

What is the role of glaciers in ice ages?

Glaciers

How do glaciers change the landscape?

How are glaciers studied?

3 Locate the information you will need.

Library

Internet

Experts

4   Organise your information using the questions you
selected as headings.

5   Make a plan.

Introduction:

Glaciers form over thousands of
years. They shape and carve the
landscape as they move.

Points in a coherent and logical sequence:

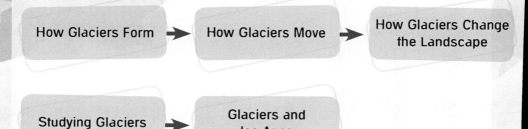

How Glaciers Form ➡ How Glaciers Move ➡ How Glaciers Change
the Landscape

Studying Glaciers ➡ Glaciers and
Ice Ages

6   Design some visuals to include in your explanation. You can
use graphs, diagrams, labels, charts, tables, cross-sections . . .

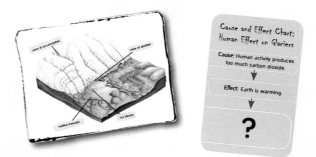

Cause and Effect Chart:
Human Effect on Glaciers

Cause: Human activity produces
too much carbon dioxide.

Effect: Earth is warming.

?

Writing an Informational Explanation...

Have you . . .

- explored causes and effects?

- used scientific and technical vocabulary?

- used the present tense? (Most explanations are written in the present tense.)

- written in a formal style that is concise and accurate?

- avoided unnecessary descriptive details, metaphors and similes?

- avoided author bias or opinion?

Don't forget to revisit your writing. Do you need to change, add or delete anything to improve your explanation?